Before you start your journey with reaching your higher self

Read with caution

Please don't take this the wrong way, if you're not going to put in the work, commit to yourself or believe you can change your narrative. You might as well put this book the fuck down, it's not for you.

Self-journaling is a labor of love mentally, physically and spiritually. I know your wandering why I didn't say emotionally, unfortunately we must take emotions out of the equation sometimes, dealing with people and even when you're self-healing. We must learn how to not give or breathe life into people, situations or past and future experiences. Many times, things don't mandate that we give it life after its over or have begun. Live in the moment

Forgive yourself for your shortcomings, know that it's okay to not have it all figured out. Be open minded while growing and glowing. Take it one level at a time, be willing to peel off layers of yourself to allow growth. Love yourself throughout your journey good and bad. Experience, create and be okay with your own existence and not another soul on this planet

KEEP PUSHING FORWARD

D1565872

ACT OF KINDNESS

I'm getting straight to the point with this section

Its not always about YOU

Did you all hear me? Or do I need to say it louder?

Good, you heard me correctly, YOU shouldn't be the only person you care about on this planet. Yes, value yourself, because when you do others will too. Being kind to others isn't just for them but for you as well. It teaches us to be more compassionate, selfless and be a positive force in the universe. Sad to Say we are reared to only love and care for people in our lives with titles. There's no truth in that at all being kind isn't essential to having personal relationships, monetary acts or the end of the world. Act of kindness can be a smile, polite greeting compliments, holding a door, listening with no intent to reply, being resourceful when you CAN without looking for anything in return. It won't ever cost you anything to be nice to another human being. I really need everyone to make a choice to treat someone that you don't know kind just because you can. It won't damage you or your body to treat someone as you would treat yourself. What you put into the universe will always came back to you good or bad. Your option to be benignant to others will lead you to be more loving to yourself. When you love and value yourself unconditionally, it makes caring for others so much easier. Because you know it doesn't cost you a dime to be kind.

Weekly Goals

Weekly Affirmations

My Week

MONDAY

TUESDAY

WEDNESDAY

THURSDAY

FRIDAY

SATURDAY

SUNDAY

Monthly Goals

Travel The World
Where Are You Going?

Keep Pushing Forward

Keep Pushing Forward

Keep Pushing Forward

Keep Pushing Forward

Keep Pushing Forward

Keep Pushing Forward

Keep Pushing Forward

Keep Pushing Forward

Keep Pushing Forward

Keep Pushing Forward

Keep Pushing Forward

Keep Pushing Forward

Keep Pushing Forward

Keep Pushing Forward

Keep Pushing Forward

Keep Pushing Forward

Keep Pushing Forward

Keep Pushing Forward

Keep Pushing Forward

Keep Pushing Forward

Keep Pushing Forward

Keep Pushing Forward

LEAD YOURSELF

LOVE YOURSELF

CHOOSE YOURSELF

HONOR YOURSELF

DON'T YOU EVER GIVE UP ON YOUR SELF

KEEP PUSHING FORWARD

-DANA BULLARD

"Other people's opinion of you does not
have to become your reality."

- Les Brown

"The graveyard is the richest place on earth, because it is here that you will find all the hopes and dreams that were never fulfilled, the books that were never written, the songs that were never sung, the inventions that were never shared, the cures that were never discovered, all because someone was too afraid to take that first step, keep with the problem, or determined to carry out their dream."

- Les Brown

"You don't have to be great to get started, but you have to get started to be great."

– Les Brown

"Most people fail in life not because they aim too high and miss, but because they aim too low and hit."

– Les Brown

Mental Check

ts normal to not be you 365 days, but it's a must to take time for you and your mental health. What you think, what you imagine and what you dream will be your results. Make them positively and aligned for your life not for anybody else. When you fall short you can't fall apart. Pick yourself up, be kind and accountable, all while healing and growing. Glowing mentally should be your new goal to reach. It's okay to go through emotional episodes, but you cannot stay there. Read it again, I said go through it, not live there. We tend to give energy, breathe air and emotions to

- » people
- » materials things
- » situations
- » relationships

and jobs that are no longer essentially needed. In other words, be mindful what you put inside your thoughts, your mind is precious. Learn to be gentle with it, learn to decompose the waste in your mind. If its trash throw it away.

If you keep trash in your house for days, weeks, months or years, what will happen?

Answer this question in your journal section, before reading on.

Okay, SO YOU GET IT NOW your mind shouldn't be containing garbage.

Throw that shit AWAY

Make it normalize to go through things, but don't you ever stay there. Treat your mind like you treat your outer appearance. If you're not right internally, no matter how much Fenty, designer labels, 33 inches, close fades with the crisp line, mink lashes or surgeries you get it will NOT fix your inner. Do your interior work than your exterior won't require so much labor. LIVE and make choices for YOU. Make mental self-care a priority in your daily routine. Meditation is great for a good release.

LET IT GO

Research mental exercises and see what works for you.

To love your mental, is to love yourself wholeheartedly.

- » LOVE YOUR MIND
- » LOVE YOUR SELF
- » IT'S TO LOVE YOUR PEACE

Weekly Goals

Weekly Affirmations

My Week

MONDAY

TUESDAY

WEDNESDAY

THURSDAY

FRIDAY

SATURDAY

SUNDAY

Monthly Goals

_____

_____

_____

_____

_____

_____

_____

_____

_____

_____

_____

_____

_____

_____

_____

_____

_____

_____

_____

_____

_____

_____

_____

_____

_____

_____

Travel The World
Where Are You Going?

Keep Pushing Forward

Keep Pushing Forward

Keep Pushing Forward

Keep Pushing Forward

Keep Pushing Forward

Keep Pushing Forward

Keep Pushing Forward

Keep Pushing Forward

Keep Pushing Forward

Keep Pushing Forward

Keep Pushing Forward

Keep Pushing Forward

Keep Pushing Forward

Keep Pushing Forward

Keep Pushing Forward

Keep Pushing Forward

Keep Pushing Forward

Keep Pushing Forward

Keep Pushing Forward

Keep Pushing Forward

Keep Pushing Forward

Keep Pushing Forward

"Live out of your imagination instead of out of your memory."

– Les Brown

"Formal education will make you a living; self-education will make you a fortune.

-Jim Rohn

"Motivation is what gets you started.
Habit is what keeps you going."
- Jim Rohn

"If you don't design your own life plan, chances are you'll fall into someone else's plan. And guess what they have planned for you? Not much."

- Jim Rohn

"If you don't like how things are, change it. You are not a tree."

- Jim Rohn

Travel/Explore/ Create Memories

Traveling goes hand and hand with growth and healing.

Why, do I say that?

Because for me traveling over the years gave me a different perspective on life. It allowed me to see things not with my traditional lens or mindset, but from other with non-similar traditions, food, languages, fashion, moral and beliefs. It helped a lot with being open minded, which led to trying new things such as different cultural foods, learning about traditions that I never heard of or participated in.

Did it ever dawn on you that you only live on a tiny piece of the world? Something to think about, right?

So that means we didn't experience life as much as we thought. Honestly, we are completely blind to the world and all its wonder. It was created to explore, experience, enjoy and REPEAT. I told my son all his life you are not your

70

environment. Go book that trip, stop complaining about the price, stop creating reasons to not go. Because at the end of the day you have money for takeout, debt, bills, designer labels, entertainment and what ever else you like doing. You better make sure that traveling is included in your life budget. Get your ass up and out of your comfort zone. Time to traverse the world and learn to appreciate living more than traditions, create your own traditions that are aligned with you and your loved one's existence. Step outside your conditioned movements.

Remember Dana told you that.

In this section to manifest your journey to travel, explore, experience and create memories all around this huge place called the world.

Weekly Goals

Weekly Affirmations

My Week

MONDAY

TUESDAY

WEDNESDAY

THURSDAY

FRIDAY

SATURDAY

SUNDAY

Monthly Goals

Travel The World
Where Are You Going?

Keep Pushing Forward

Keep Pushing Forward

Keep Pushing Forward

Keep Pushing Forward

Keep Pushing Forward

Keep Pushing Forward

Keep Pushing Forward

Keep Pushing Forward

Keep Pushing Forward

Keep Pushing Forward

Keep Pushing Forward

Keep Pushing Forward

Keep Pushing Forward

Keep Pushing Forward

Keep Pushing Forward

Keep Pushing Forward

Keep Pushing Forward

Keep Pushing Forward

Keep Pushing Forward

Keep Pushing Forward

Keep Pushing Forward

Keep Pushing Forward

"We must all suffer from one of two pains: the pain of discipline or the pain of regret. The difference is discipline weighs ounces while regret weighs tons."

- Jim Rohn

"Discipline is the bridge between goals and accomplishment"

– Jim Rohn

"All the people in your life are truly doing the best they can with what they have. People can only love you to the capacity that they are able to love themselves. They can only forgive and embrace you to the capacity that they are able to forgive and embrace themselves. They can only give you what they have the capacity to give. You may think that you deserve more, and you may be correct. But that means nothing if a person simply doesn't have the ability to give it to you."

- Lisa Nichols

"Self-enrichment is that act of creating a thousand micro wins, so you can have one macro win."

- Lisa Nichols

"When you give yourself permission to have made mistakes in the past—when you begin to trust yourself about making new choices—that's when your intuition becomes reliable and trustworthy."

- Lisa Nichols

FORGIVENESS

What does forgiveness mean to you?

Do you forgive for yourself or others?

Forgiveness is a conscious, deliberate decision to release feelings of resentment or vengeance toward a person or group who has harmed you, regardless of whether they deserve your forgiveness.

Let me say this forgiveness is for you and only you, not the person who did you wrong, who broke your heart or even let you down. You will be the only one who will benefit from being accountable for you. Accountability leads to forgiveness; to forgive others you must forgive yourself first. Forgiveness takes some deep digging, hard commitment, dedication and self-love to achieve. Why should you carry that heavy load around with you?

We do it unconsciously, not acknowledging that we carry so much shit that includes our own and from others that we dump on ourselves. Stop being a human dumpster and collecting bullshit you don't need; the dumpster even gets dumped once a week. What are you doing with your BULLSHIT? You're not getting paid to collect unvaluable energy, words, people opinions, and uncertainties. It doesn't benefit you in no way. Let it go

I learned that trauma causes drama, if you know what I mean.

In other words, trauma is associated with hurt. You heard of the old saying "Hurt people hurt people". Its so much truth in that statement. If you think about it whenever you have experienced hurt, it was caused by someone who was hurting. You can't always see people's pain, because we become actors and actresses at a very young age. We are taught not to express our feelings. Do as you told, not what you think or feel that's right. We cover up so much pain that it becomes a part of our makeup, awhile camouflaging the scars, cuts and bruises caused by others and self-sabotaging behavior. Learn to be less abusive to yourself, be more compassionate about how you love yourself.

Weekly Goals

Weekly Affirmations

My Week

MONDAY

TUESDAY

WEDNESDAY

THURSDAY

FRIDAY

SATURDAY

SUNDAY

Monthly Goals

Travel The World
Where Are You Going?

Keep Pushing Forward

Keep Pushing Forward

Keep Pushing Forward

Keep Pushing Forward

Keep Pushing Forward

Keep Pushing Forward

Keep Pushing Forward

Keep Pushing Forward

Keep Pushing Forward

Keep Pushing Forward

Keep Pushing Forward

Keep Pushing Forward

Keep Pushing Forward

Keep Pushing Forward

Keep Pushing Forward

Keep Pushing Forward

Keep Pushing Forward

Keep Pushing Forward

Keep Pushing Forward

Keep Pushing Forward

Keep Pushing Forward

Keep Pushing Forward

"Comparison is and will always be

the thief of all joy."

- Lisa Nichols

"Your story is important."

- Lisa Nichols

All you need is the plan, the road map, and the courage to press on to your destination."

- Earl Nightingale

"People with goals succeed because they know where they're going."

- Earl Nightingale

"We can let circumstances rule us, or we can take charge and rule our lives from within."

-Earl Nightingale

SELF-CARE/HEALTH

The most important section of the journal....

**Why do you think self-care is and
should be very salient in your everyday life?**

Think about this question because your answer will be your solution. Rather it guides you to self-care or self-sabotaging behavior it's your choice. Always chose yourself.

Your health and self-care are a very important pieces to your puzzle, without it you won't never be whole. People is fast to chase money, popularity and approval of others, not realizing that your health is wealth. I know it sounds cliché', but it's so much truth in it. The way you view yourself is the way you will treat yourself. Make it the norm to love all over you unapologetically. Peace is your objective in life. No matter what you must do to obtain peace, you do it. People will make you feel bad for loving YOU, don't fall for it. In life if you do not take care you, not another will do it for you. No matter what title they have in your life. Don't cheat yourself. You weren't created to cheat yourself out of living life abundantly. Take time for YOU. Go enjoy self-care activities, yes, they exist and its ok to partake in them.

- » Massages/Spa
- » Hiking/Explore Nature
- » Traveling
- » Meditation
- » Beauty Salon/Barbershop
- » Manicures and Pedicures
- » Facials
- » Be Spontaneous /Try Something New
- » Take care of your body, it's your wealth

Exercise (I'm not a pro at this yet, but I know it's an important part of growth lol)

Me Time (Use this time to learn yourself)

I just named a few, but you get the picture.

For once in your existence just put you first without feeling guilty, shorted or unfulfilled. You won't miss out on much by doing so. LOVE YOU WITH NO LIMITS

Weekly Goals

Weekly Affirmations

My Week

MONDAY

TUESDAY

WEDNESDAY

THURSDAY

FRIDAY

SATURDAY

SUNDAY

Monthly Goals

Travel The World
Where Are You Going?

Keep Pushing Forward

Keep Pushing Forward

Keep Pushing Forward

Keep Pushing Forward

Keep Pushing Forward

Keep Pushing Forward

Keep Pushing Forward

Keep Pushing Forward

Keep Pushing Forward

Keep Pushing Forward

Keep Pushing Forward

Keep Pushing Forward

Keep Pushing Forward

Keep Pushing Forward

Keep Pushing Forward

Keep Pushing Forward

Keep Pushing Forward

Keep Pushing Forward

Keep Pushing Forward

Keep Pushing Forward

Keep Pushing Forward

Keep Pushing Forward

"Everything begins with an idea."

-Earl Nightingale

"What's going on in the inside shows on the outside."

- Earl Nightingale

"You are, at this moment, standing, right in the middle of your own acres of diamonds."

-Earl Nightingale

Made in the USA
Middletown, DE
07 May 2022